Aliaksandr Sukhanevich

The Russian Cruiser
Askold

KAGERO

Starboard side view.

1st Class Protected Cruiser Askold

In the late 1890s the Russian Empire sought to strengthen its presence in the Far East, China and Korea. Faced with a growing threat posed by the Imperial Japanese Navy, the Russians saw an urgent build-up of their naval forces in the region as an utmost priority. On February 20, 1898 Emperor Nicholas II approved a supplementary shipbuilding program "for the Far East", which would see the construction of six 5,000 – 6,000 ton cruisers, in addition to ships already being built under the 1895 program. The task to formulate technical requirement for the new vessels was delegated to the Maritime Technical Committee (Russian: MTK).

Design stage

The requirements drafted by the MTK were based on the key premise: the future cruiser was to be more powerful and faster than her Japanese counterparts built in England, or their British equivalents. The required speed was set at 23 kt. The ship was to be armed with 12 152 mm main guns, license-built at Obukhov plant based on the original design of the French engineer Canet. Secondary battery was to consist of twelve 75 mm guns, in addition to small caliber weapons. The ship was expected to have a range of 5,000 NM at cruising speed. Due to small displacement, heavy armament and the need to carry substantial fuel reserves, the new ship would have no armor belt, but only armored main deck.

In early April Russian and foreign shipyards received invitations to bid for the contract. However, the contract to build *Varyag* – the first ship of the series (which tentatively consisted of three vessels) was awarded outright to William Cramp & Sons Co. from Philadelphia. In July 1898 Kiel-based Germania (part of Krupp) was selected to deliver the second cruiser (future *Askold*). After the tender was closed, two more bids came in, one of which came in from Vulcan Stettin. The Vulcan's design was viewed as superior to the Germania's bid and the shipyard was awarded the contract to build the third cruiser in the series – *Bogatyr*. The best ship to emerge from the competition was to become the lead ship of the new class of cruisers.

Construction and trials

The contract was formally signed on August 4, 1898. The shipyard received 3.78 million rubles to build the warship within 23 months of signing the contract. The shipyard's management took it upon themselves to deliver "the best Russian cruiser" built by a foreign shipyard. Unfortunately, in their quest for speed (the ship was to be capable of top speed of 23 kt – quite an impressive figure in those days) the engineers ended up with the hull design that was too narrow and too light.

The construction began on October 24, 1898, even before the technical drawings could be formally approved. On December 21, 1898 the cruiser was named after the legendary 9th century Varangian prince of Kiev, *Askold*. On January 11, 1899 the ship was officially entered into the navy register as a 1st class cruiser. The ship was launched on March 2, 1900 and on April 11, 1901 she put to sea for the first time. During sea trials, on September 6, the ship displacing 5,950 tons reached the average speed of 23.39 kt over four 2-mile runs. On September 15 the ship underwent official 6-hour speed trials off the island of Bornholm. During the first run she achieved the average speed of 23.59 kt, while the second run produced the average of 23.83 kt (maximum speeds

achieved during the tests were 23.98 and 24.01 kt, respectively, with machinery delivering 21,000 and 20,885 shp). The tests reveal severe vibrations in the stern section of the hull, which subsided once the structure of the hull had been strengthened. Machinery trials were performed on November 3 in the waters of Bay of Kiel. At 128 rpm the powerplant produced 23,500 shp. After 2 hours and 20 minutes of travel at full speed, the acceptance committee ended the test. The ship was officially accepted on January 6, 1902 and on January 12, with a band playing and guns firing ceremonial salutes, the Russian Imperial Navy ensign was raised for the first time.

Overview of the ship's particulars

Architecture and hull

The main differences between the new Russian cruiser and *Varyag* included covered 152 mm guns, more reliable Thornycroft-Schulz water-tube boilers and three-shaft propulsion system, not to mention her rather unique external appearance. *Askold*'s characteristic five smoke stacks earned her the nickname "packet of Woodbines" – slim cigarettes popular among British sailors. The cruiser's long and narrow hull had a length to beam ratio of 8.7. The short and heavily loaded bow section often led to the ship's "digging" into the water when sailing into the waves. Crew's living conditions with the confines of the slim hull left much to be desired, especially in combat conditions when the ship's company was typically more numerous. The hull was divided into thirteen water-tight compartments. *Askold* featured three decks: upper (9.5 mm in mid-section and 7 mm at each end), battery deck (6 mm) and armored deck. Cofferdams (0.8 m wide) extended along the entire length of the hull and reached up to 1.2 m above the waterline. Double bottom ballast space was lined with a 13 – 50 mm layer of Portland cement. Coal bunkers were placed between bulkheads 50 and 97, both below and above the armored deck, for enhanced protection.

Armament

Askold's main battery consisted of twelve 152 mm/45 Canet guns, mounted on the upper deck and forecastle. With a standard loadout the battery was designed to provide fire for up to three hours at 180 rounds per gun. The ammunition supply consisted of 564 AP shells, 564 HE rounds, 624 cast-iron shells and 372 segmented rounds. Secondary battery consisted of twelve 75 mm/50 Canet guns placed on the battery deck. The guns' loadout was sufficient for a 2.5 hour barrage at 650 rounds per gun. The ammunition supply included 1,500 AP shells, and 2,116 cast-iron rounds. *Askold* also carried eight 47 mm/43 Hotchkiss guns (six in fixed mounts and two removable weapons), in addition to a pair of 37 mm/23 Hotchkiss guns that could be mounted in picket boats. Complementing the ship's armament were two VS Baranovsky 63.5 mm/19 ship-borne assault cannons on wheeled mounts. The ship's landing party had at their disposal two 7.62 mm Maxim machine guns.

The ammunition was stowed in twelve magazines (six for 152 mm ammunition, three for 75 mm shells and three for small caliber ammunition). In total, the magazines could hold 2,204 152 mm rounds, 3,616 75 mm shells, 5,990 pieces of 47 mm ammunition and 1,620 37 mm rounds. The transport of projectiles, charges and unitary ammunition was performed via 14 elevators (eight for main battery guns and three for each 75 mm and small caliber rounds), or by hand, as a backup method.

Two Barr & Stroud rangefinders were mounted on the bridge and aft superstructure. Artillery fire was directed from the fire control station

Port side view.

equipped with an electric N.K. Geisler fire control computer. A set of six 75 cm Mangen searchlights was used to illuminate targets at night.

Askold was also equipped with six 381 mm torpedo launchers. Two fixed tubes were placed along the hull's longitudinal axis on the bow and stern of the ship. There were also four side-mounted launchers – two above the waterline and two below. The former could be traversed 45° towards the bow and 35°towards the stern. In addition, the ship carried a pair of 254 mm torpedo launchers that could be mounted on the cutters. *Askold* carried a supply of 14 torpedoes, or "Whitehead's mine" as they were often referred to at that time. The cruiser could also deploy 35 moored mines mk. 1898. To that end, a mining raft was used, which could carry up to six mines at a time.

Armor protection

Askold's armor arrangement was typical of other protected cruiser designs. Its cornerstone was the armored deck stretching across the hull, whose lower edge dropped to 1.4 m below the waterline. Over the machinery rooms, the upper edge of the horizontal section of the armored deck was at 3.9 m above the waterline. The deck's armor plating consisted of two layers: the lower layer, fabricated of 10 and 15 mm steel plates and the upper layer, consisting of 30 and 60 mm nickel-steel alloy plates. The horizontal section of the armored deck was 40 mm thick, while the sloped sections were 75 and 100 mm thick. Torpedo launchers mounted above the waterline were protected with 60 mm vertical armor, while 30 mm armored plates provided protection at the bottom and top of the tubes. The conning tower featured 150 mm armor plating (side walls and entry) and 40 mm plates on the floor and roof. An armored duct, measuring 400 mm in diameter and 80 mm in thickness, provided protection for steering lines, engine order telegraph cables and speaking tubes.

Propulsion

The cruiser was powered by three 4-cylinder vertical Germania steam engines, each driving its dedicated propeller. The machines were installed in two compartments. The forward engine room housed two

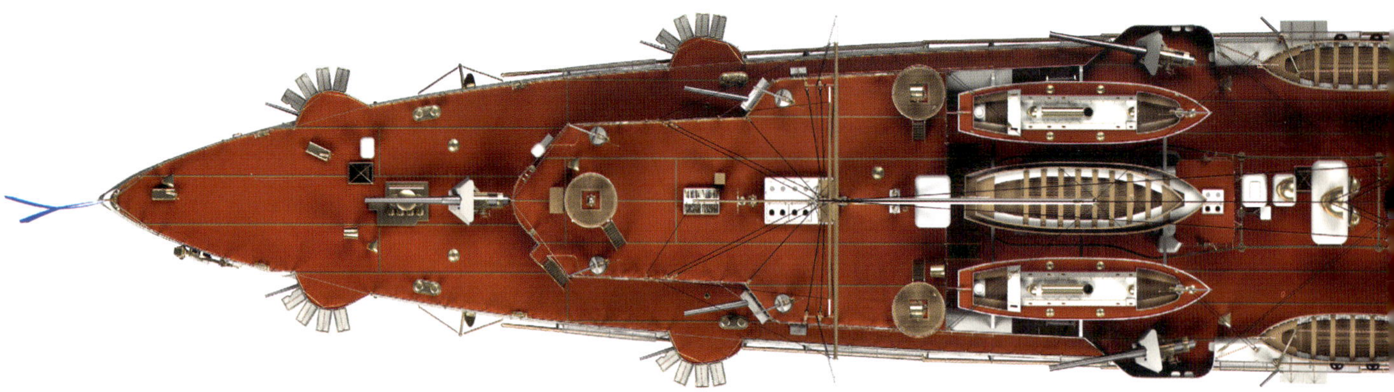

machines called "side machines". The aft compartment contained the third engine driving the middle shaft and propeller. The steam was provided by nine Thornycroft-Schulz boilers. Eight of them were installed in pairs in four boiler rooms, while the fifth compartment housed the ninth boiler. The boilers could produce steam of the maximum pressure of 17 kg/cm^2. The total available heat area was 5,020 m^2. Each boiler had a capacity of 21.2 t/h and had the coal usage of 1 kg/1 HP per hour. Standard bunker capacity of 720 tons of coal translated into a range of 2,340 NM. The boilers had one significant advantage: they took less time from initial firing to achieving full capacity than similar designs of that time. *Askold* could carry a full load of coal of 1,050 tons or maximum load of 1,250 tons. At full speed, the cruiser used 18 tons of coal per hour.

Electric power was provided by six Siemens & Halske generators with a total output of 339 kWt. The ship's 105 V DC power network provided electricity for electric engines and searchlights. The cruiser had a total of 46 electric motors: 14 for ammunition hoists, 24 running ventilators, 7 for bilge pumps and one in the ship's workshop. There were also 750 light fixtures.

Modernizations

In 1904 *Askold* was stripped of two 75 mm guns, two 47 mm Hotchkiss guns, machine guns and a pair of Baranovsky landing cannons, as well as 35 naval mines. After the Russo-Japanese war cast-iron and segmented projectiles were replaced by HE rounds. At the same time the overwater torpedo launchers were also removed from the ship. Two forward embrasures, formerly housing 75 mm guns, were welded shut. During World War I two 47 mm Hotchkiss guns were replaced by two 57 mm British AA guns and two 47 mm French AA guns, as well as four machine guns.

Ship's boats

Askold carried two steel steam cutters (12, 25 tons, 9.35 kt, 180 NM), utility launch, two picket boats and a motor cutter, as well as standard wooden yawls and whaleboats. Some of the boats could carry armament: the steel cutters could be armed with a forward-mounted 47 mm Hotchkiss gun and a 7.62 mm Maxim machine

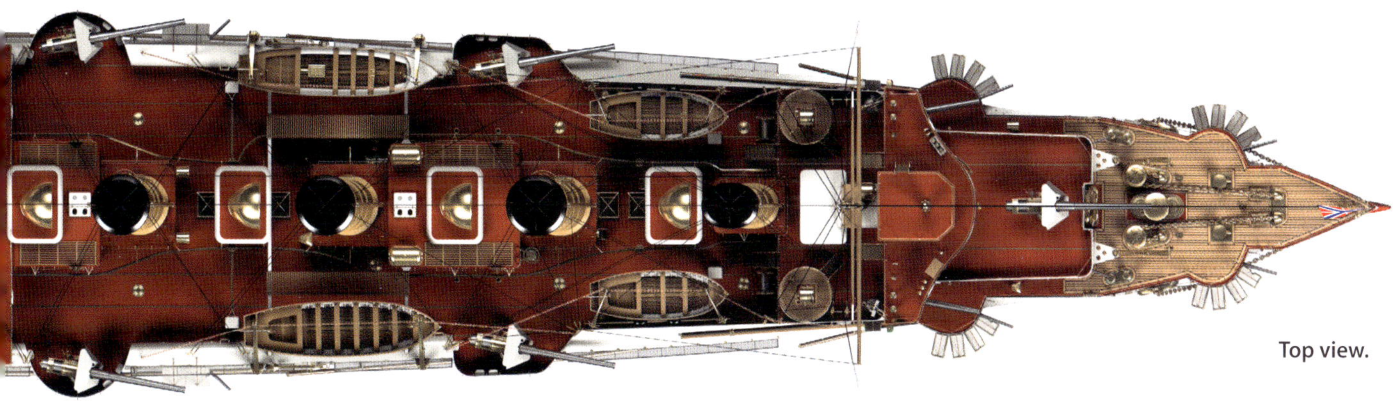

Top view.

Bow view.

gun on the stern (a 254 mm torpedo launcher could be mounted instead of the Hotchkiss gun); the launch could transport a 63.5 mm/19 Baranovsky landing cannon; and picket boats could be armed with 37 mm/23 Hotchkiss gun.

Ship's company

When *Askold* entered service, her standard crew consisted of 21 officers, 9 warrant officers and 550 NCOs and enlisted personnel. During World War I the ship's company increased to 650, including 19 officers. Crew quarters were located on the accommodation deck and in the aft section of the armored deck. The accommodation deck housed a sick bay, pharmacy, galley, bath and the ship's Orthodox chapel.

Operational service

After a short deployment to the Baltic, *Askold* was ordered to the Far East. During the transit from Kiel to Algiers the cruiser remained under the watchful eye of Lt Col A.N. Krilov – the MTK representative, whose job was to monitor the hull's performance in blue water operations, using purpose-built instrumentation of his own design. During the Russo-Japanese war *Askold* took part in the defense of Port Arthur, providing support to reconnaissance operations, as well as naval mining missions. On August 10, 1904, after the Battle of the Yellow Sea, the cruiser managed to make her way to Shanghai, where she was subsequently stripped of her armament and interned by the Chinese government. On June 6, 1906 *Askold* became part of the Siberian Flotilla. On October 17, 1907 some of the ship's crew took part in the uprising in Vladivostok. In the aftermath, seven crew members were executed by firing squad, while the ship's skipper, charged with dereliction of duty, shot himself. Between January 1, 1911 and November 1912, *Askold* underwent a major refit in Vladivostok, which included the replacement of all water tubes in her boilers and installation of new plating of the double bottom.

In the early days of World War I *Askold*, along with the cruiser *Zhemchuk*, became part of the Allied joint task force tasked with pursuing German cruisers operating in the Indian Ocean and in the waters of South-East Asia. In late 1914 the ship deployed to the Mediterranean, where she operated off the coasts of Palestine and Syria. On December 16, 1914 *Askold* sank a German transport *Peter Rickmers* (5,162 BRT) and a Turkish gun boat *Seddülbahir*. A day before, on December 15, her crew boarded and captured a Turkish freighter *Haife* (1,790 BRT). Between March 5, 1915 and January 22, 1916 the cruiser took part in the Anglo-French Dardanelles operation. From March 15, 1916 till January 9, 1917, *Askold* remained docked at Toulon, France, for a major machinery overhaul, which also included the replacement of deck plating and the main battery guns. While the ship was docked, there was an explosion in one of the ammunition magazines, whose cause couldn't be established. In the end, eight of the crew members were charged with sabotage and four of them, despite the lack of clear evidence of any wrongdoing, were shot.

On December 5, 1916 *Askold* became part of the Arctic Ocean Flotilla. During the passage to the North, the cruiser encountered a major storm and suffered heavy damage. She sought refuge in Devonport, where emergency repairs were carried out. On June 30, 1917 *Askold* finally arrived in Kola Bay and on November 8, 1917 she formally joined the Arctic Ocean Flotilla. On July 12, 1917 the ship was seized by the British in Kola Bay and joined the Royal Navy as HMS *Glory IV*. In 1919 the cruiser arrived in Britain. In 1922 British government offered to return *Askold* to the new Soviet government, but since the cruiser was in a state of disrepair, she was sold for scrap and towed off to Hamburg, Germany.

Weight distribution of protected cruiser *Askold*

Component	Weight, t	Displacement, %
Hull	2,300	38.3
Machinery	1,270	21.2
Standard bunker	720	12
Armor	705	11.8
Armament	585	9.7
Supplies	420	7
Total:	6,000	100

Technical and tactical characteristics of cruisers built under the 1898 program

	Askold	*Varyag*	*Bogatyr*
Displacement, t normal full	 6,135 •	 6,500 7,022	 6,865 7,428
Dimensions, m	131.2/130lw x 16.87 x 6.22	129.8/127.9lw x 15.85 x 5.9	134.19 x 16.6 x 6.3
Power output, HP	19,000(23,500)	15,925	203,70
Number of boilers	9	30	16
Max speed, kt	23.8	23.2	23.5
Bunker, t normal full max	 720 1,050 1,250	 770 1,250 1,350	 • • 1,220
Range NM/wkt	2,340/22	3,682/10	4,900/10
Armament	12 x 1-152, 12 x 1-75, 8 x 1-47; 6 x 1-381 WT	12 x 1-152, 12 x 1-75; 6 x 1-381 WT	2 x 2 + 8 x 1-152, 12 x 1-75, 8 x 1-47; 4 x 1-457 WT
Crew	580	580	573

Key characteristics of *Askold's* artillery

Parameters/caliber	152 mm	75 mm	47 mm	37 mm
Barrel length/cal.	45	50	43	23
Barrel length, mm	6,858	3,750	2,045	842
Type of breechblock	piston	piston	falling block	falling block
Maximum elevation, degrees	20	20	10*	11
Maximum range, cables	63	42	25	15
Muzzle velocity, m/s	790	820	701	440
Rate of fire, rounds/min.	6	8	19	20
Gun and mount weight, t	13.5	2.9	0.8	0.17
Weight of AP shell, kg	45	4.9	1.5	0.5
Weight of propellant charge, kg	12.9	1.6	0.4	0.035

*+ 25°, in some sources

Stern view.

Overall view of the ship, starboard side.

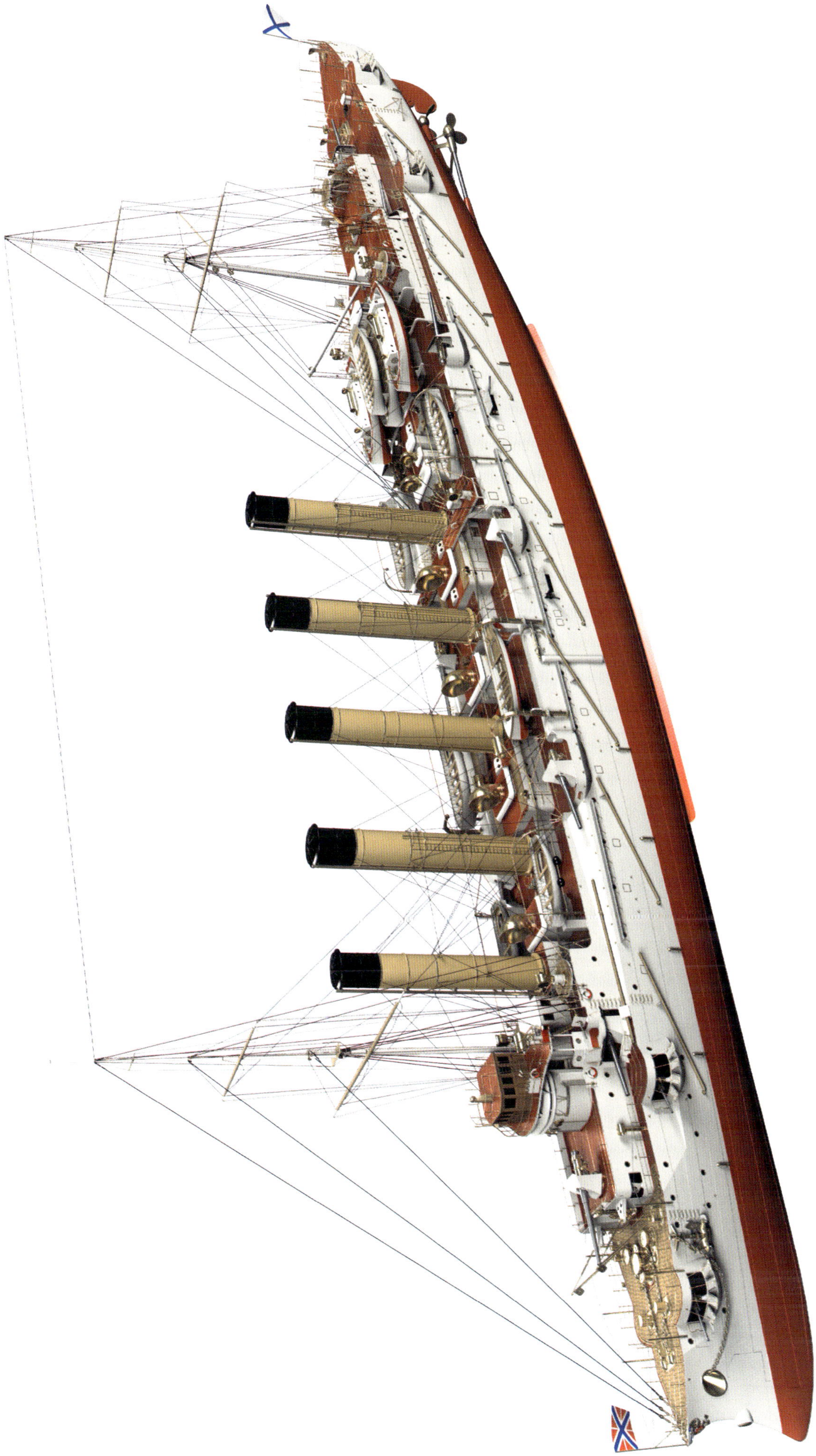

Overall view of the ship, port side.

Overall view of the ship from the bow, port side.

Overall view of the ship from the stern, starboard side.

Bow decoration of the ship.

View of the bow of the ship, starboard side.

View of the bow superstructure, starboard side.

View of the conning tower, starboard side.

View of the bow of the ship, starboard side.

View of the conning tower, starboard side.

View of the bow casemate of the 6-inch gun, starboard side.

View of the bow sponsons of 3 inch guns, starboard side.

View of the on-board installation of a 6-inch gun, starboard side.

View of the on-board installation of a 6-inch gun, starboard side.

View of the searchlight bridge, starboard side.

View of the lifeboat, starboard side.

View of the steamboat, starboard side.

View of the steamboat and lifeboats, starboard side.

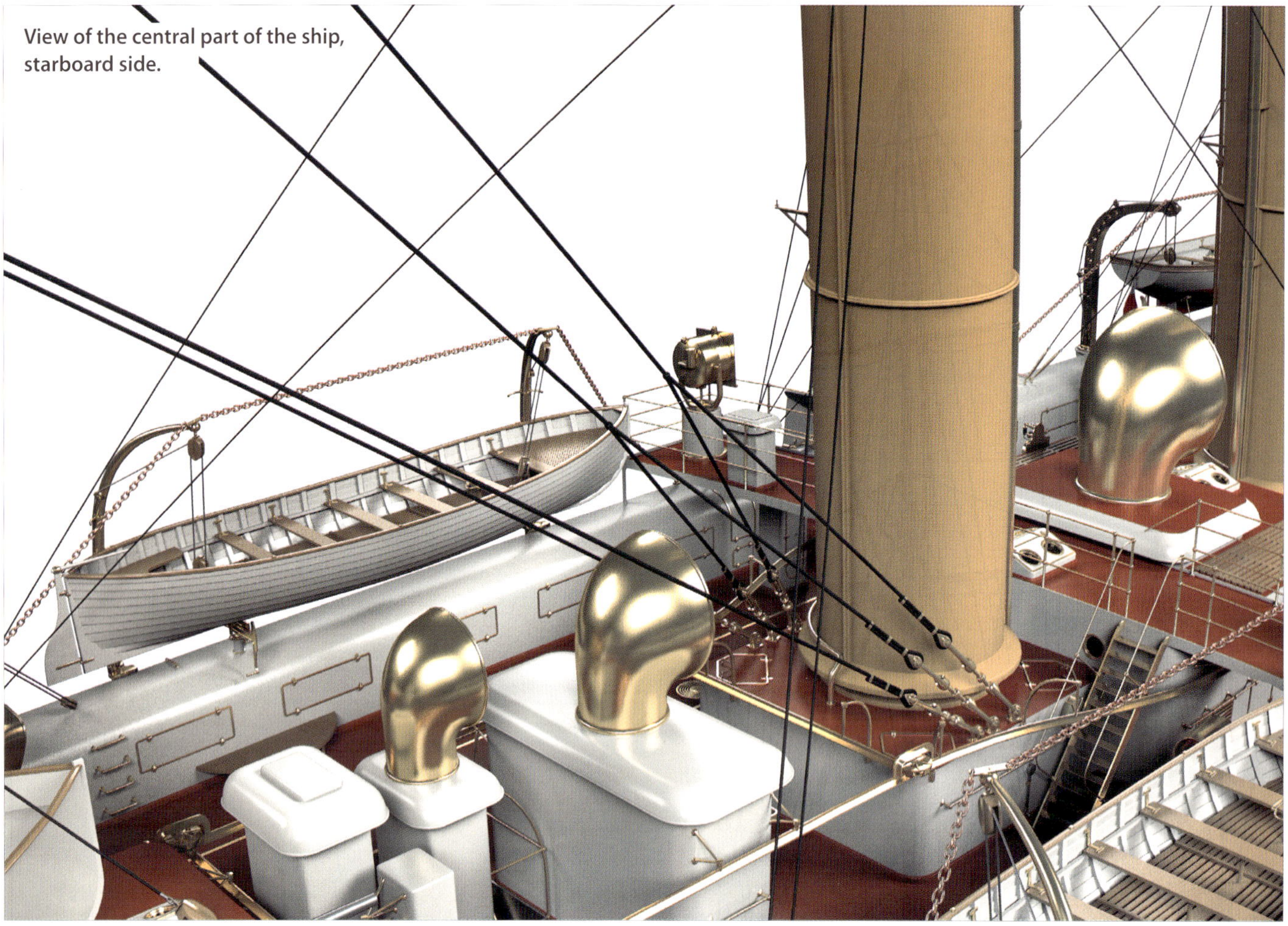
View of the central part of the ship, starboard side.

View of the steamboat and lifeboats, starboard side.

View of the stern casemate of the 6-inch gun, starboard side.

View of the stern superstructure, starboard side.

View of the stern 6 inch gun, starboard side.

View of the stern casemate of the 6-inch gun, starboard side.

View of the stern superstructure, starboard side.

View of the stern superstructure, starboard side.

View of the stern superstructure, starboard side.

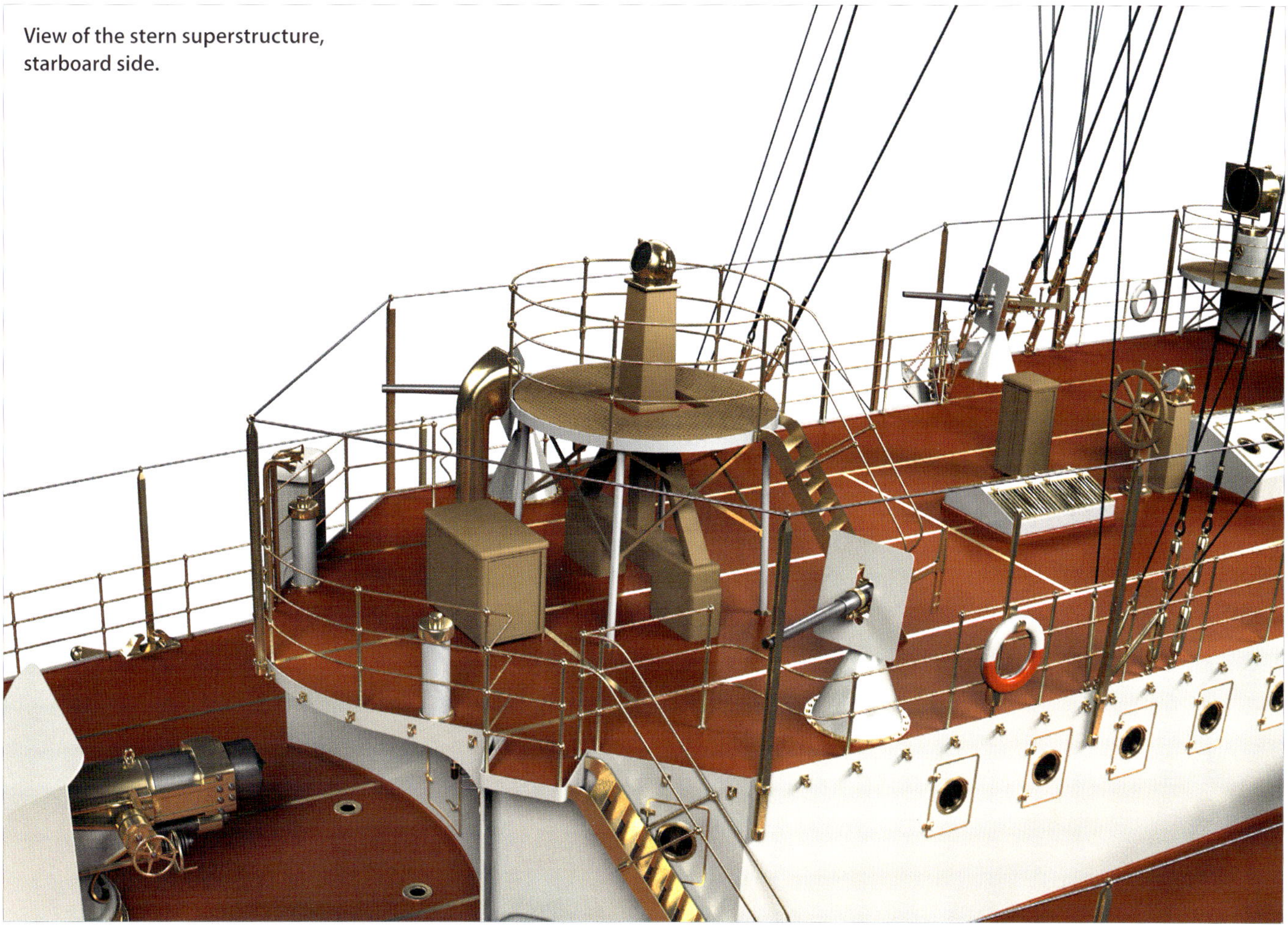

View of the stern part of the ship, starboard side.

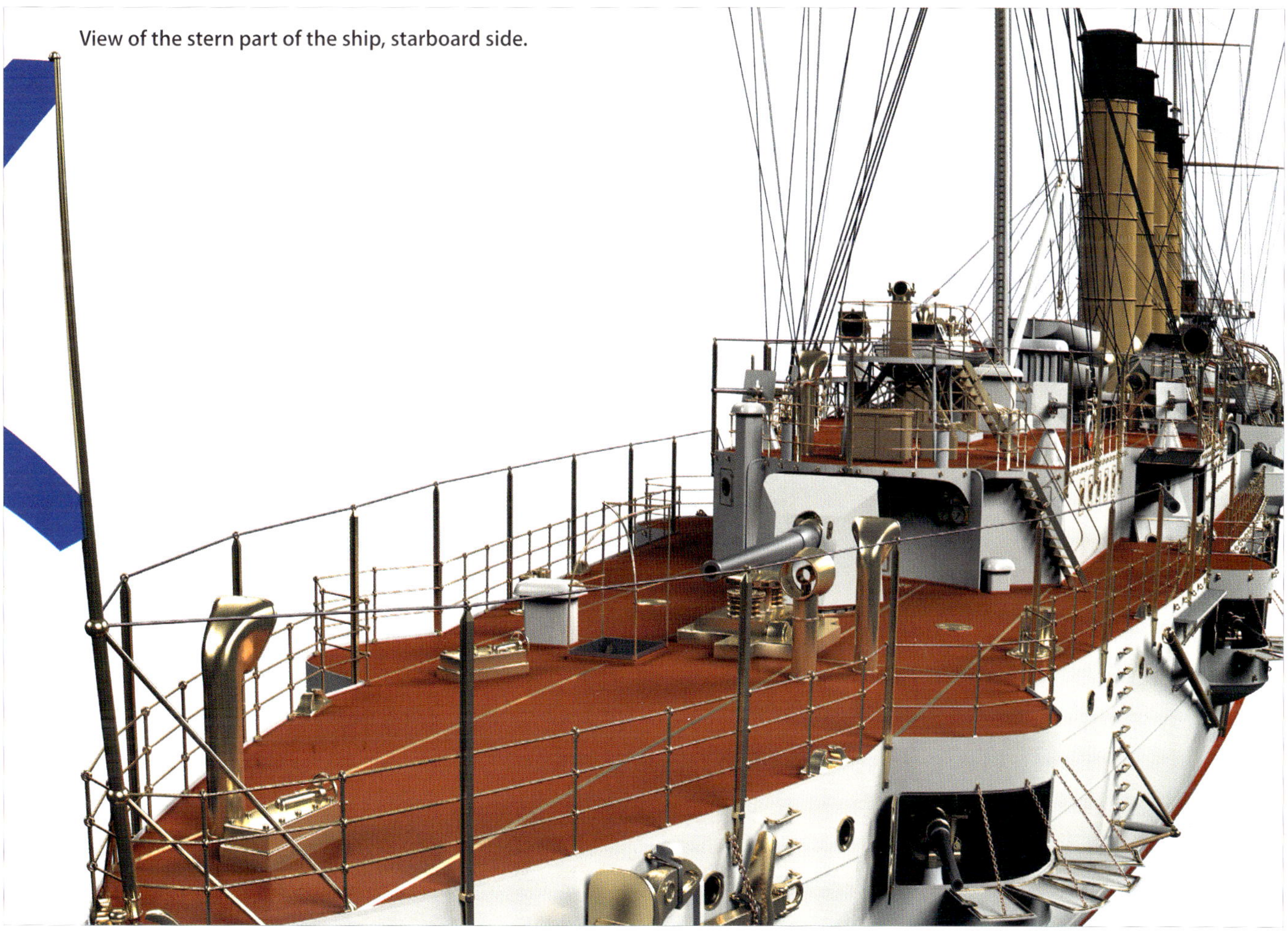

View of the stern part of the ship, starboard side.

View of the stern sponson of the 3-inch gun, starboard side.

View of the stern sponson of the 3-inch gun and the spare anchor, starboard side.

Stern decoration of the ship.

View of the starboard side of the ship.

View of the starboard side of the ship.

View of the starboard side of the ship.

View of the starboard side of the ship.

Overall view of the bow part of the ship, starboard side.

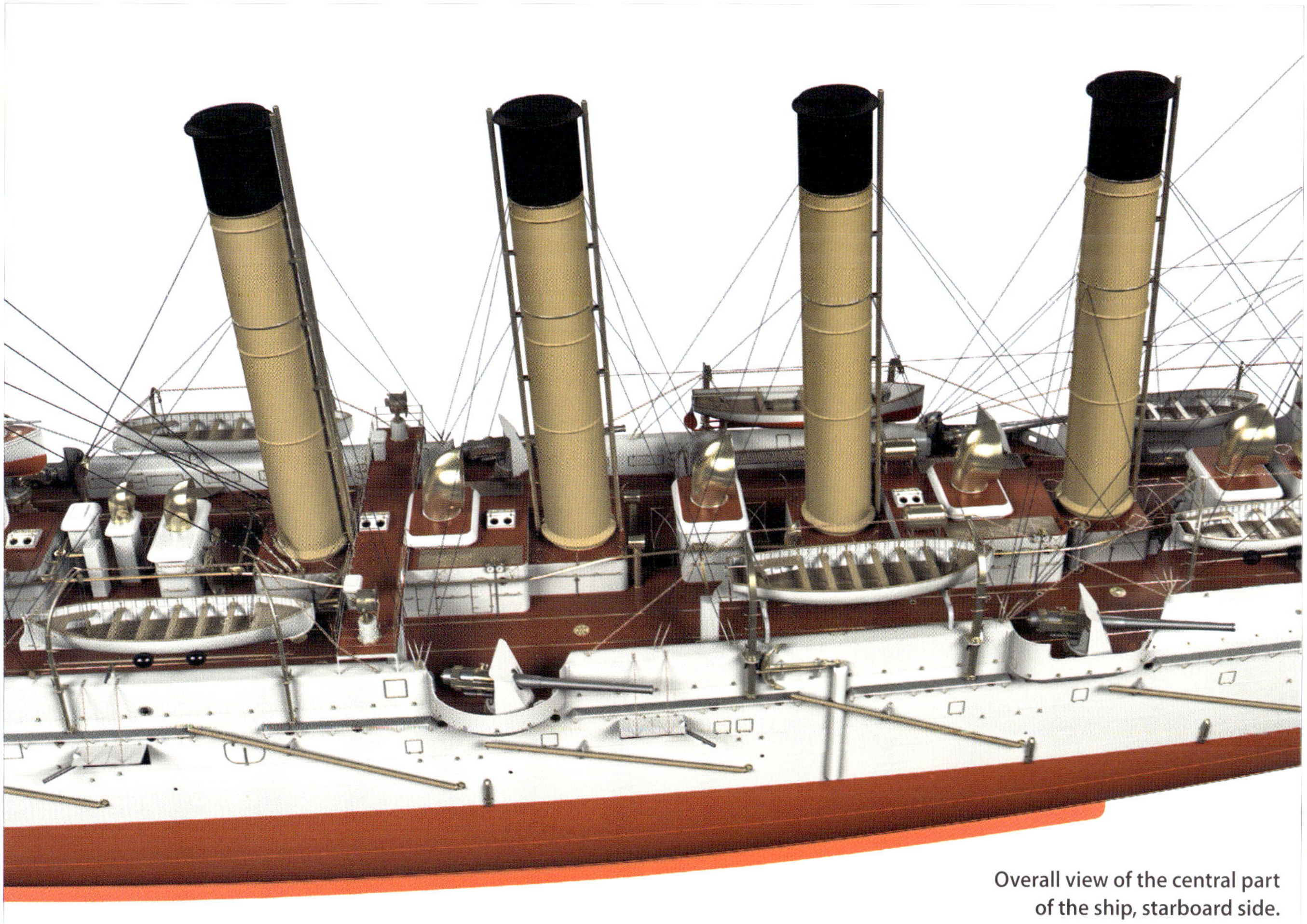

Overall view of the central part of the ship, starboard side.

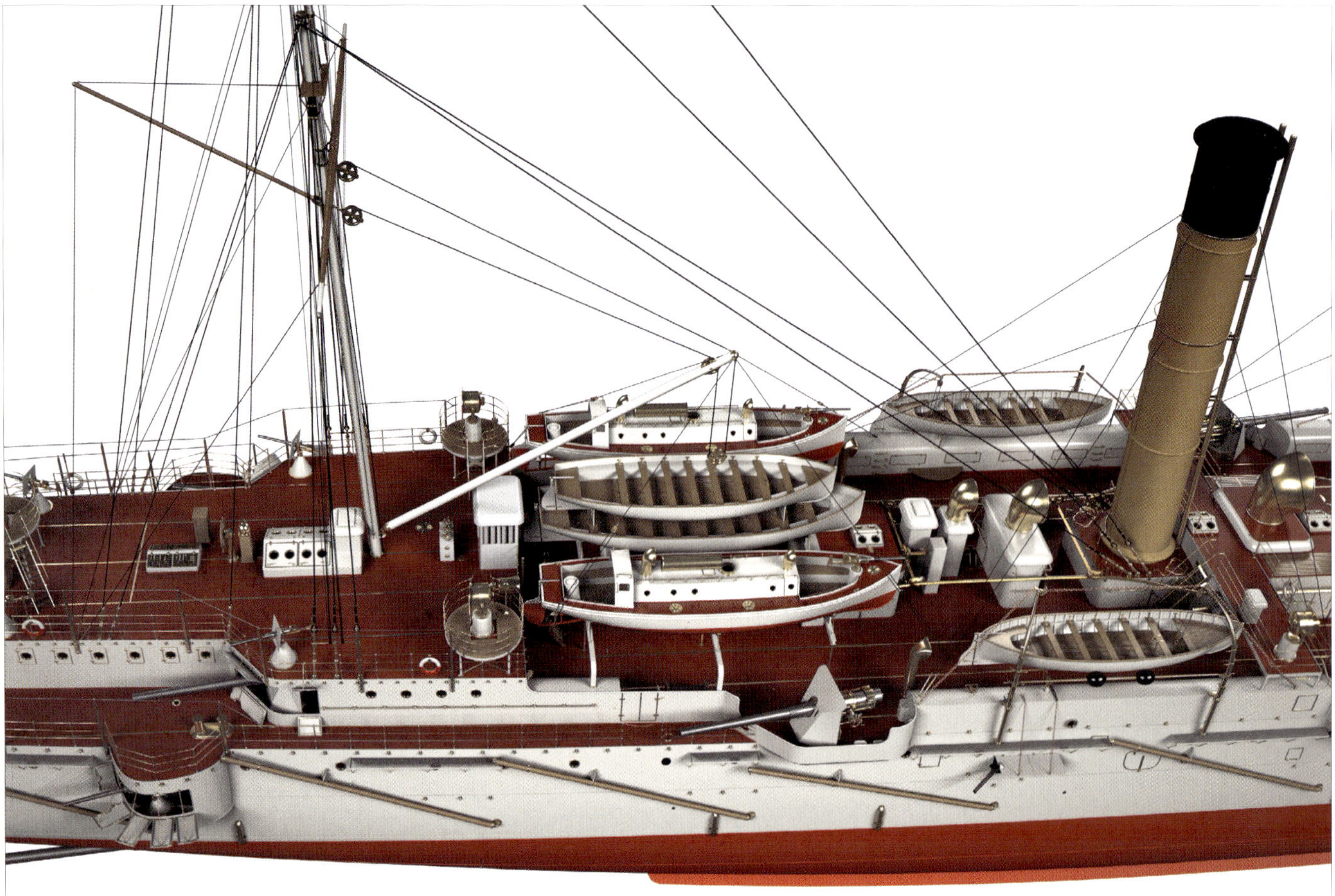

Overall view of the central part of the ship, starboard side.

Overall view of the stern part of the ship, starboard side.

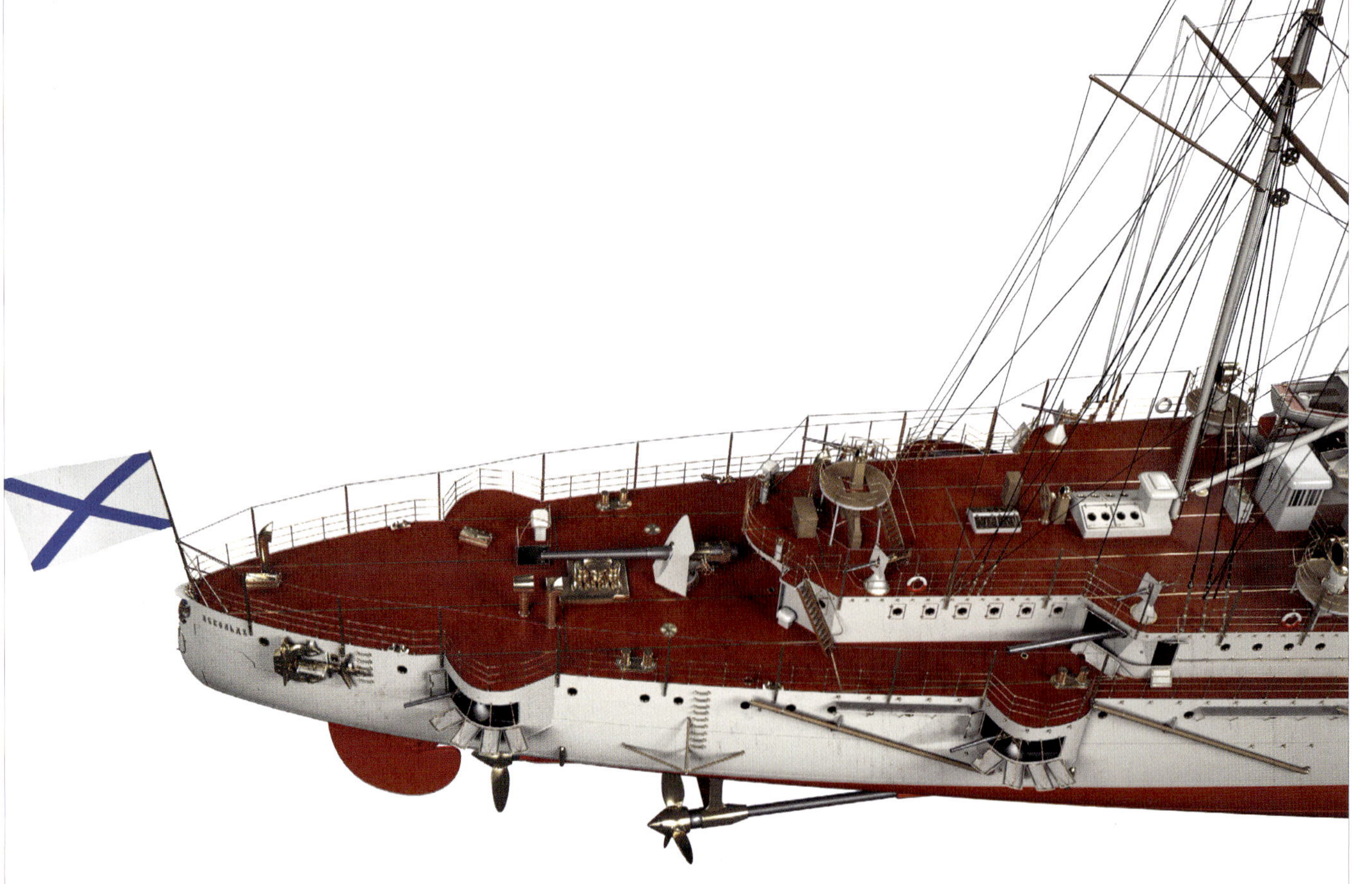

Stern decoration of the ship.

View of the stern part of the ship, port side.

Overall view of the ship from the stern, starboard side.

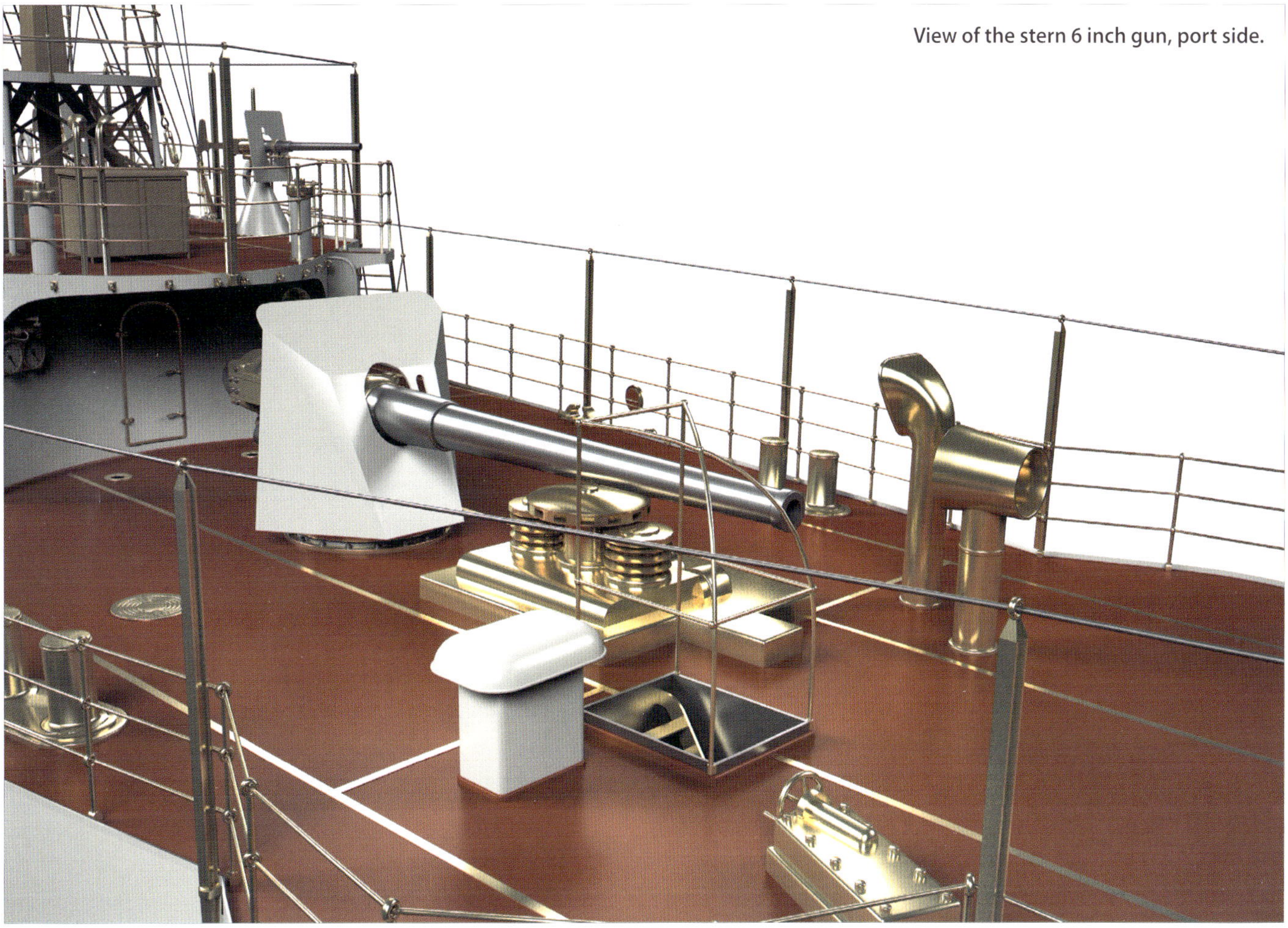

View of the stern 6 inch gun, port side.

View of the stern superstructure, port side.

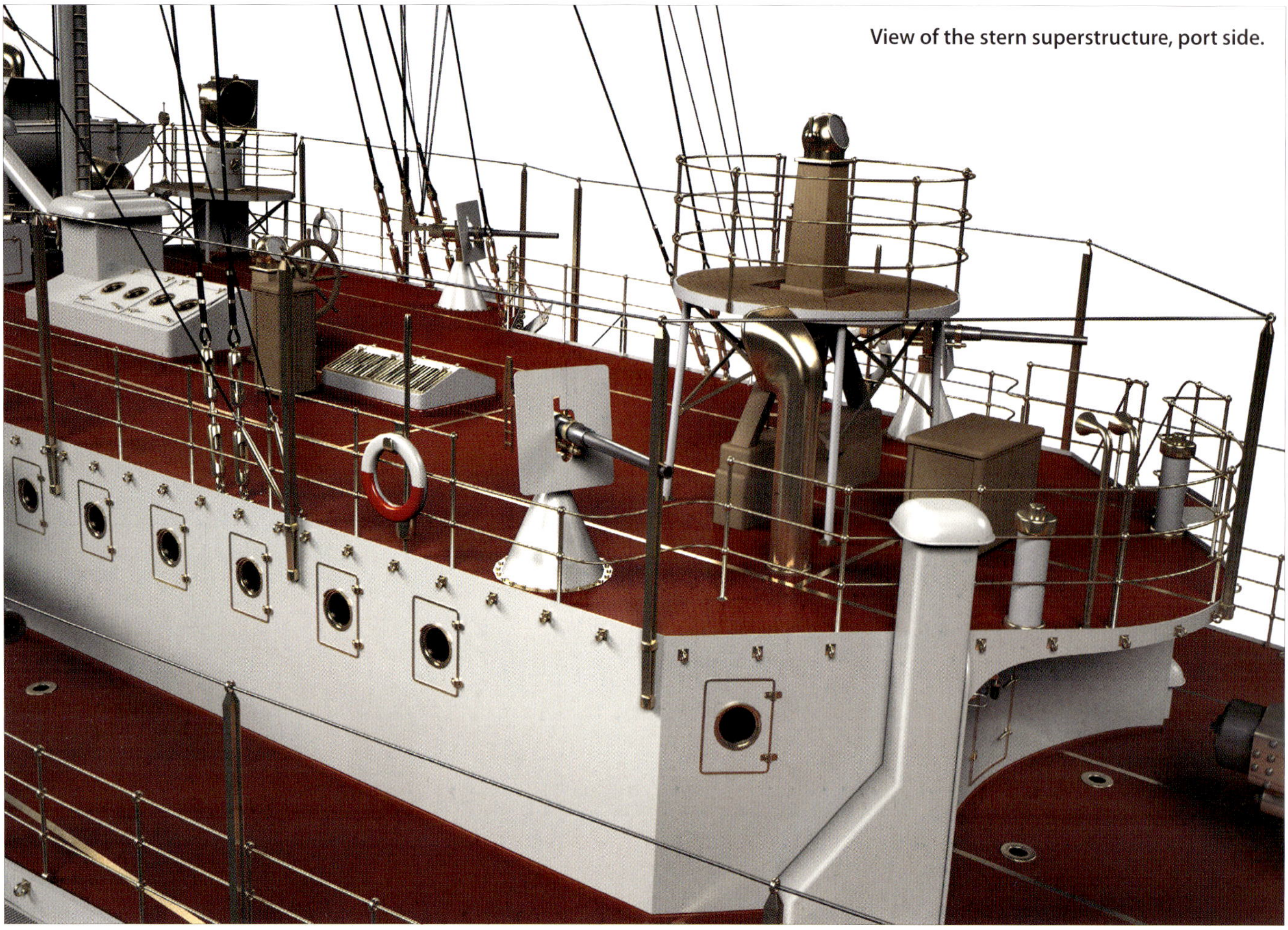
View of the stern superstructure, port side.

View of the stern superstructure, port side.

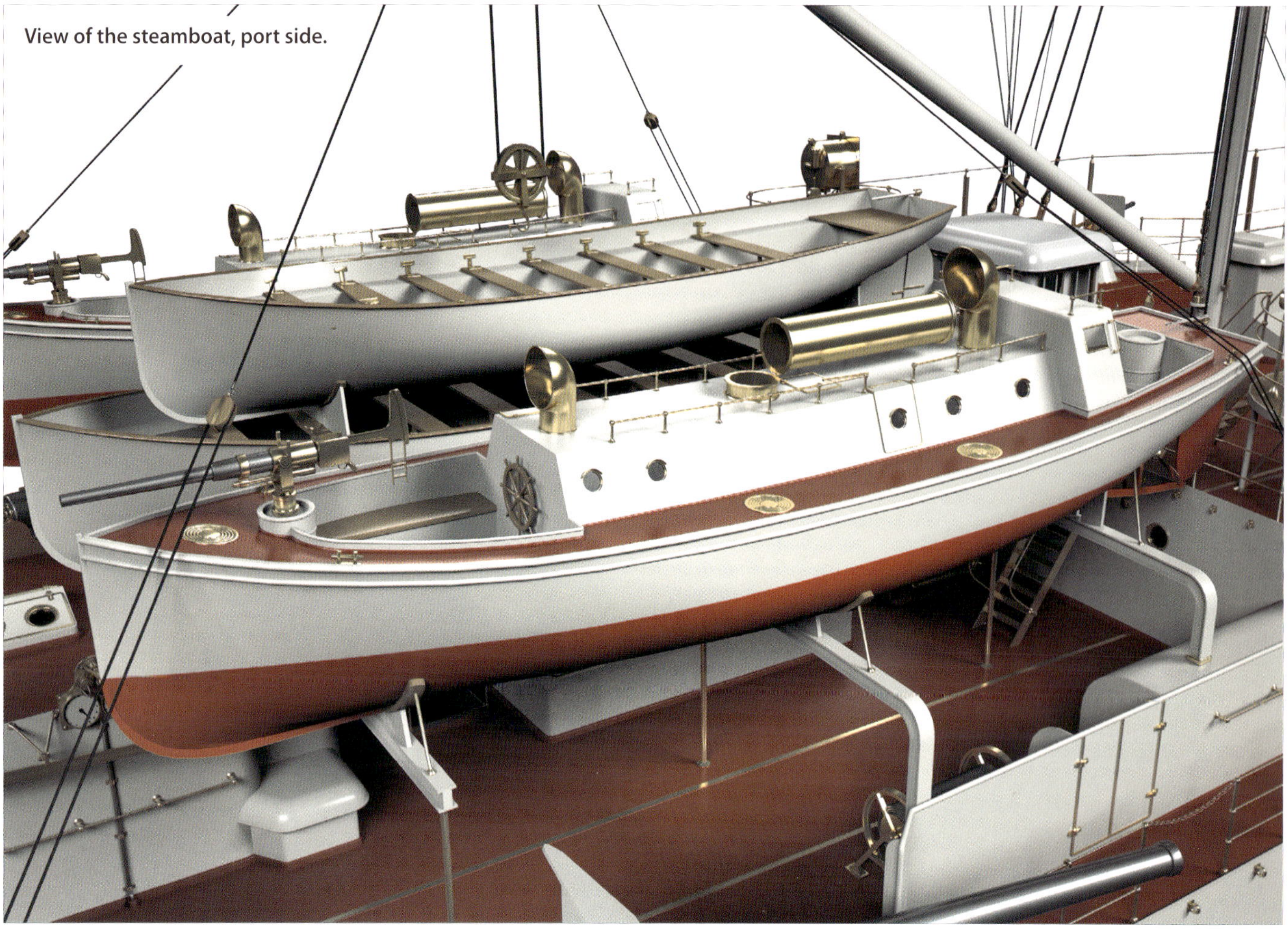

View of the steamboat, port side.

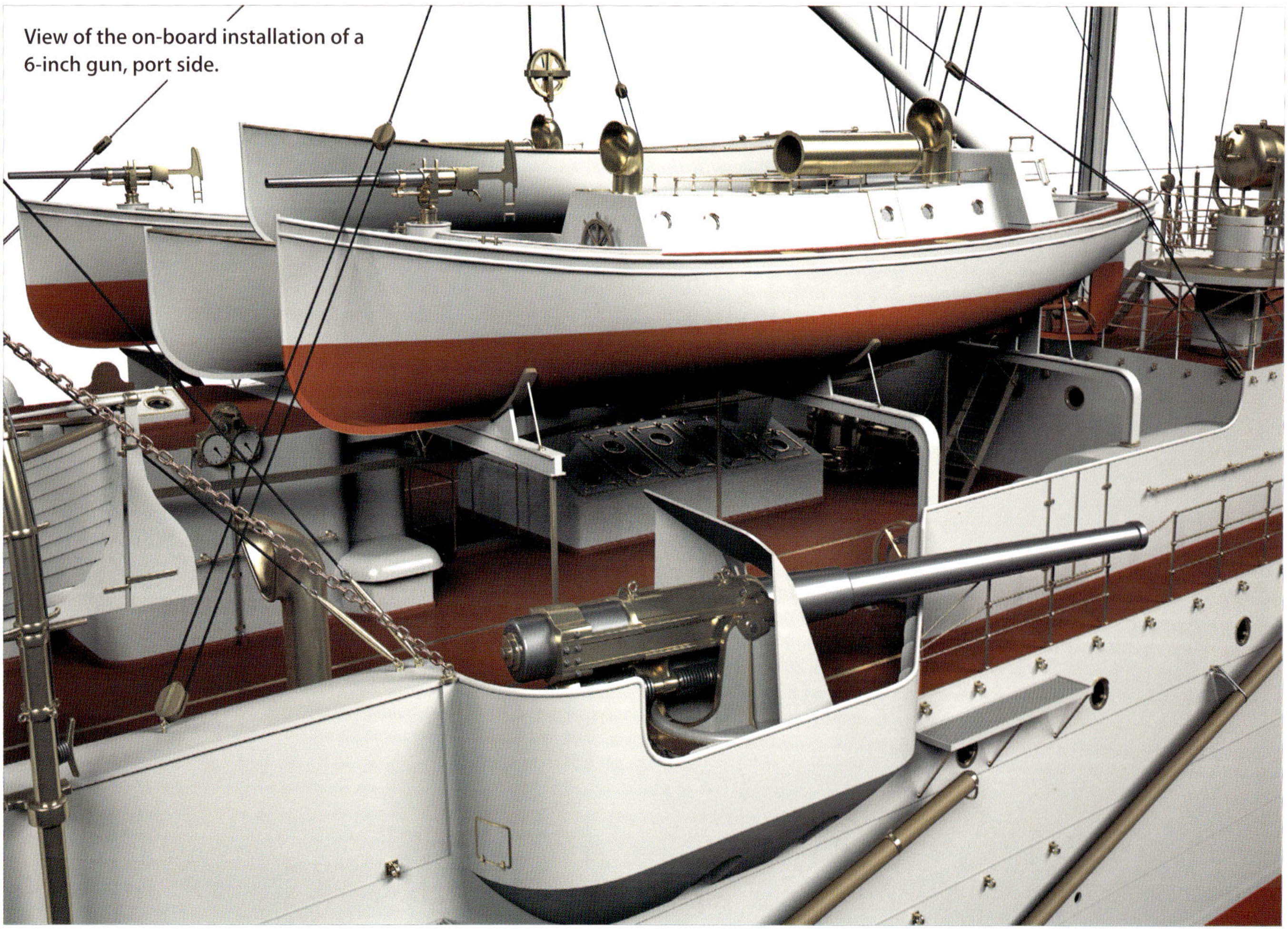

View of the on-board installation of a 6-inch gun, port side.

View of the central part of the ship, port side.

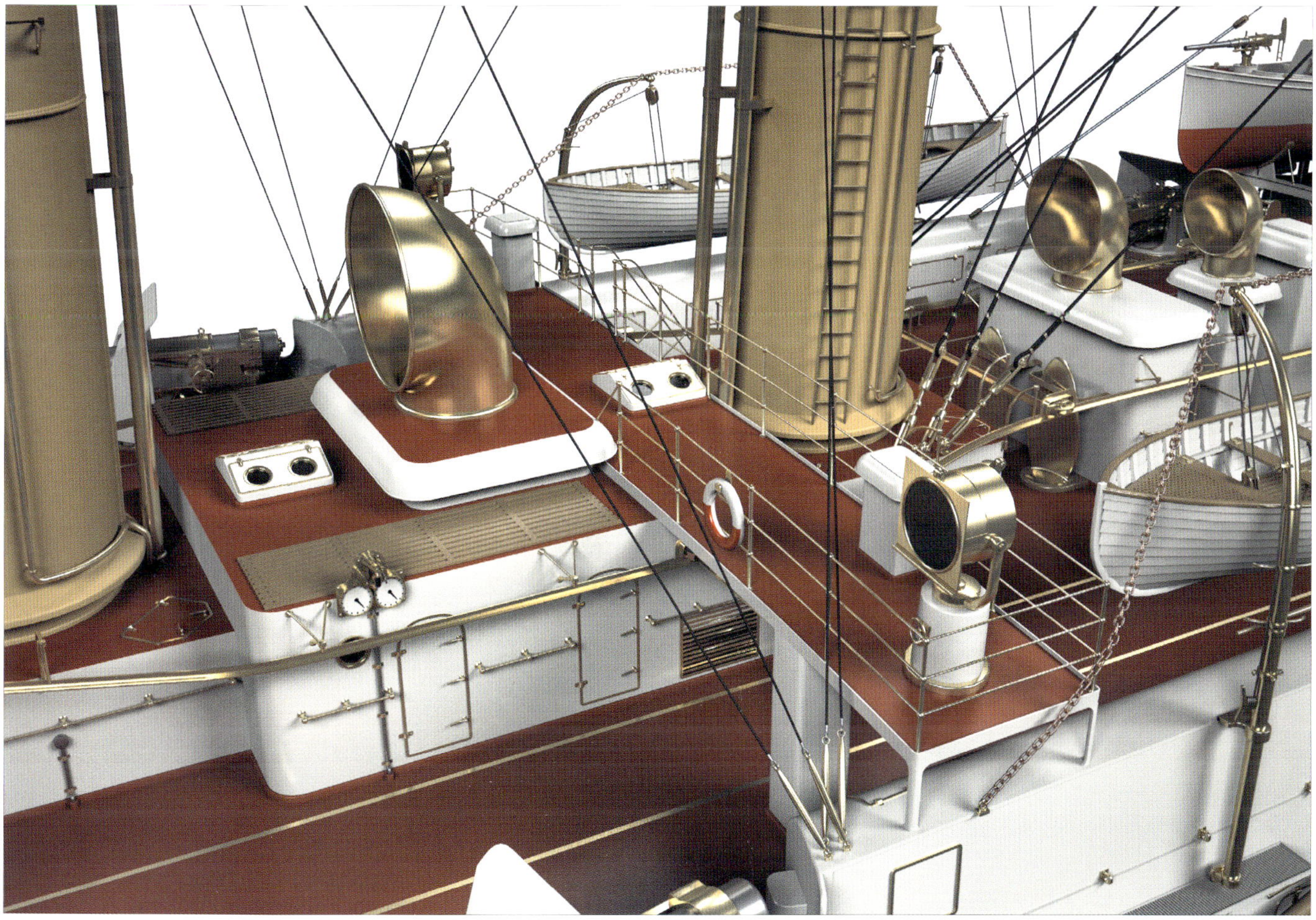
View of the searchlight bridge, port side.

View of the central part of the ship, port side.

View of the funnel, port side.

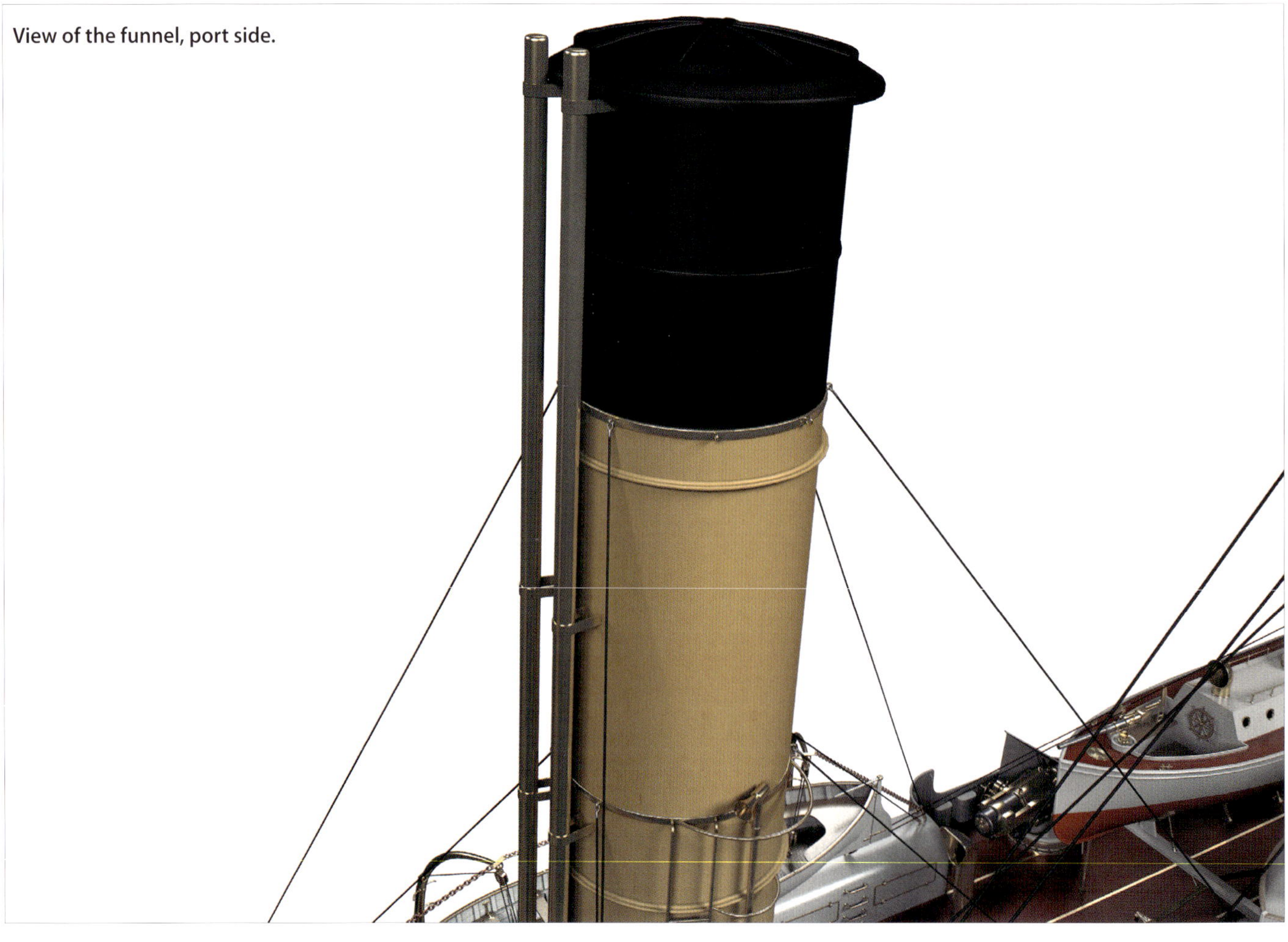

View of the funnel, port side.

View of the mainmast, port side.

View of the central part of the ship, port side.

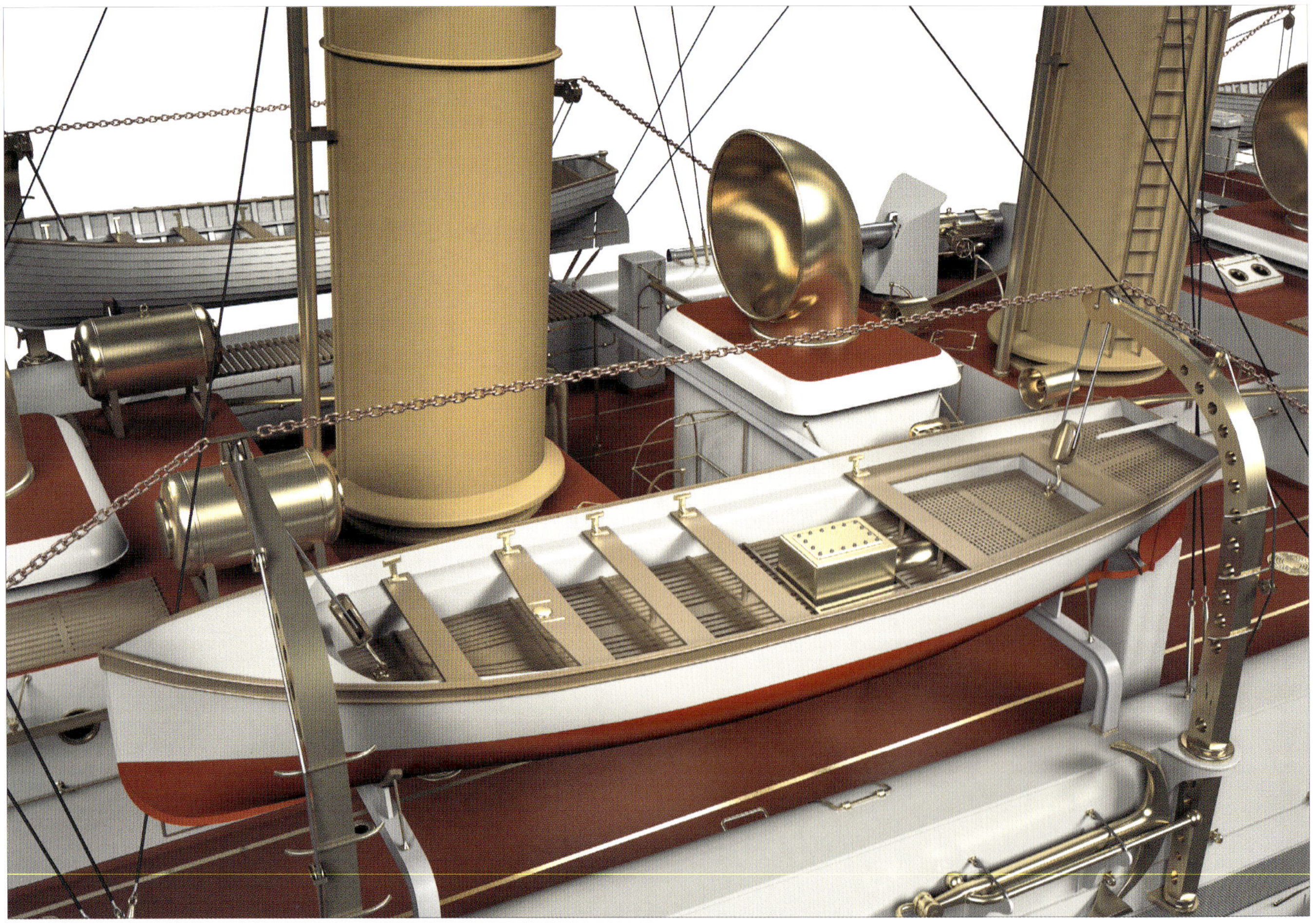
View of the motor boat, port side.

View of the central part of the ship, port side.

View of the on-board installation of a 6-inch gun, port side.

View of the lifeboat, port side.

View of the bow casemate of the 6-inch gun, port side.

View of the bow superstructure, port side.

View of the bow superstructure and a bow 6 inch gun, port side.

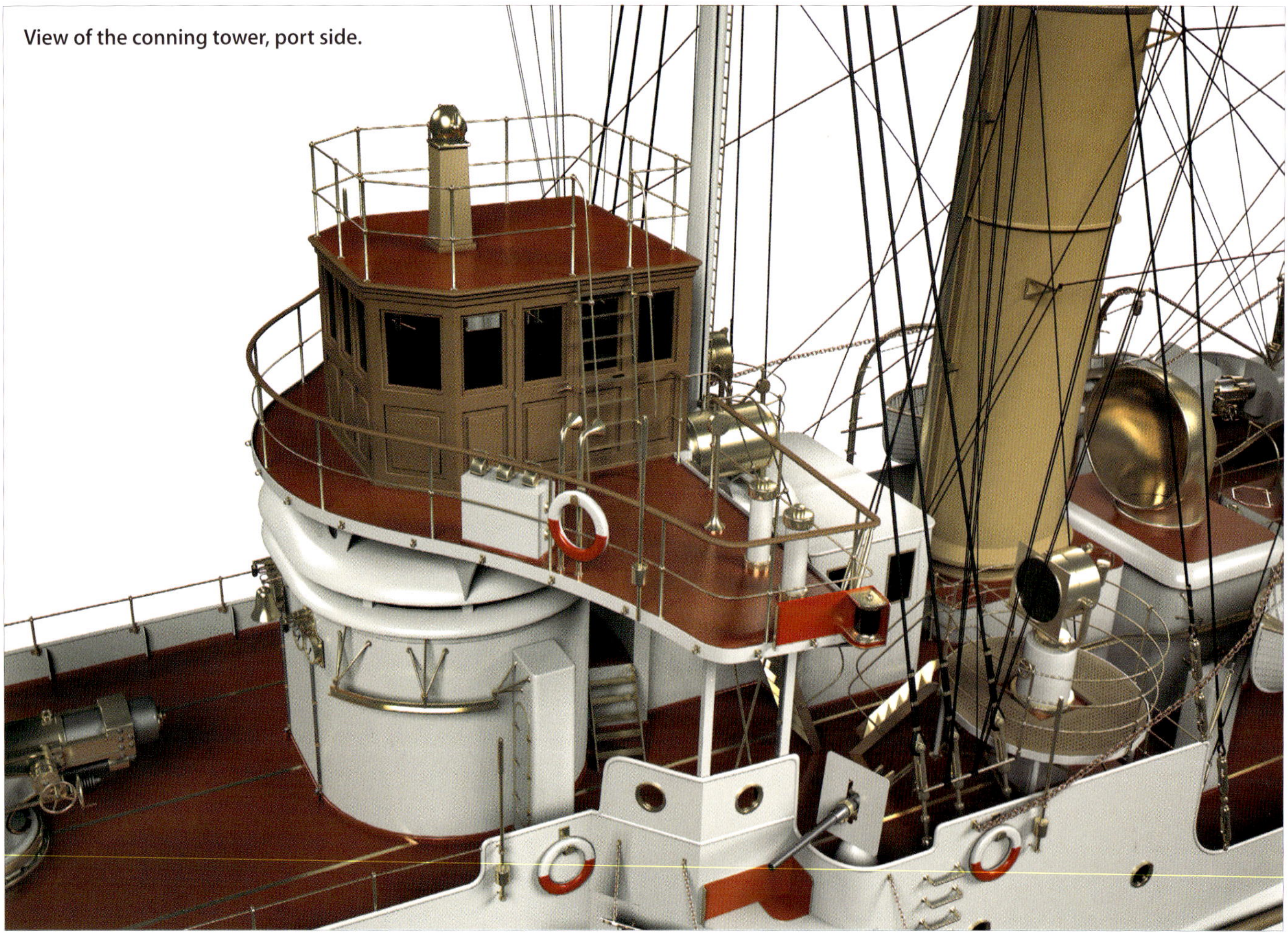
View of the conning tower, port side.

View of the conning tower, port side.

View of the bow 6 inch gun, port side.

View of the bow superstructure, port side.

View of the bow superstructure, port side.

View of the port side of the ship.

View of the port side of the ship.

View of the port side of the ship.

View of the port side of the ship.

View of the port side of the ship.

View of the Anchor Hill, port side.

View of the bow of the ship, port side.

View of the funnels, port side.

View of the searchlight bridge, starboard side.

View of the searchlight bridge, starboard side.

View of the on-board installation of a 6 inch gun, starboard side.

View of the central part of the ship, starboard side.

View of the lifeboat, starboard side.

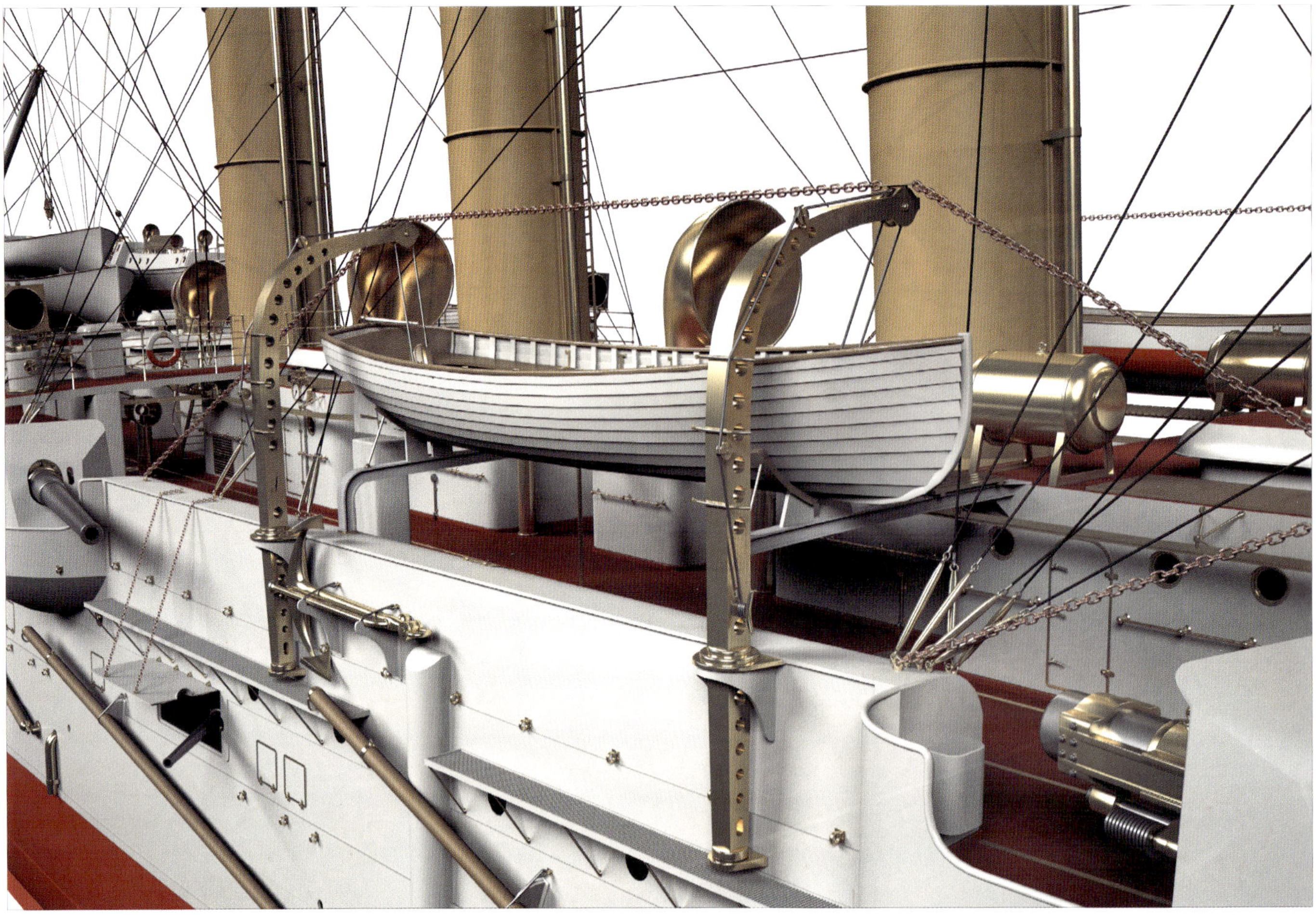
View of the central part of the ship, starboard side.

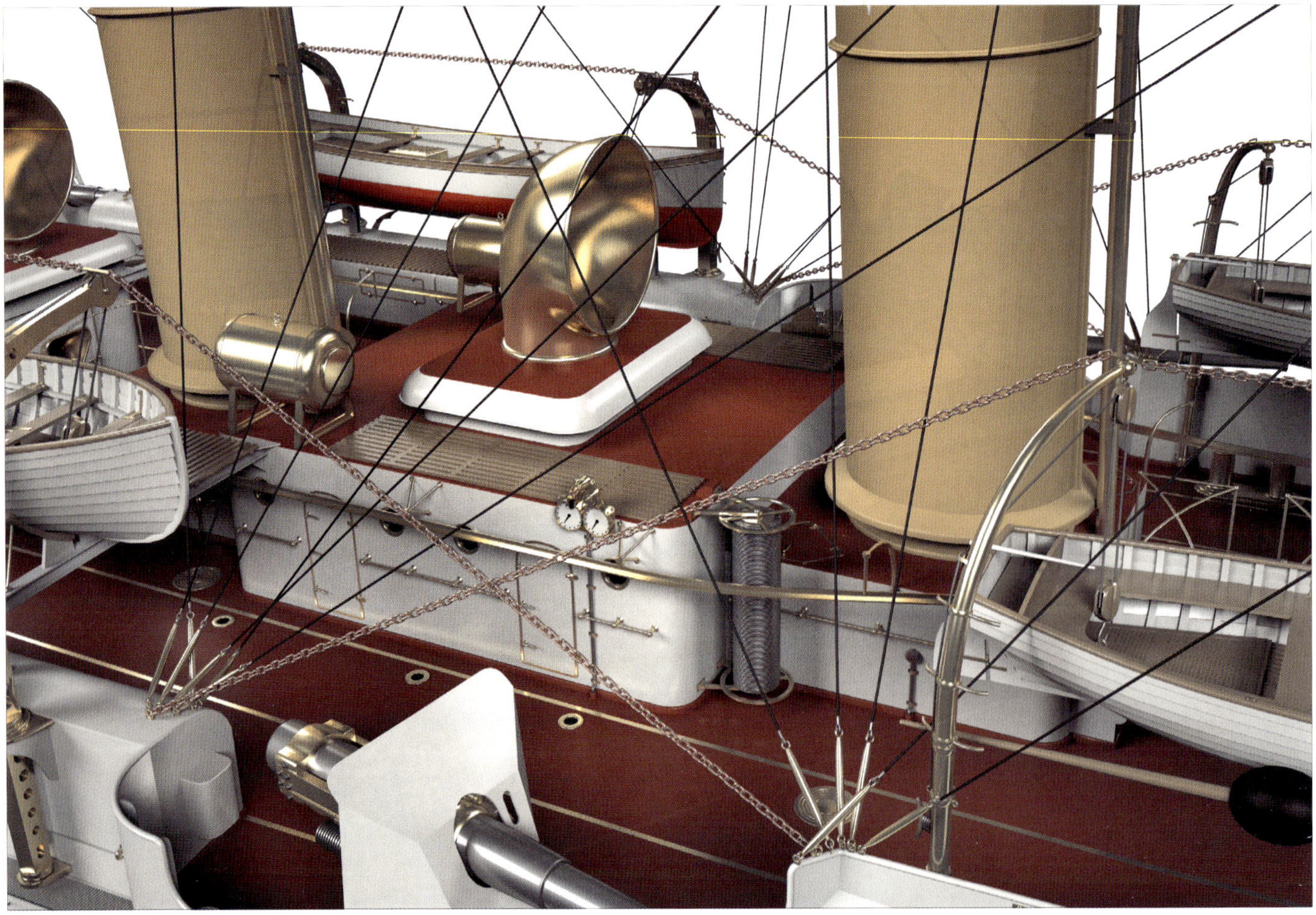
View of the on-board installation of a 6-inch gun, starboard side.

View of the lifeboat, starboard side.

View of the bow casemate of the 6-inch gun, starboard side.

View of the foremast, starboard side.

Steam boat.

Steam boat.

Motor boat.

Motor boat

6 inch Canet gun.

6 inch Canet gun.

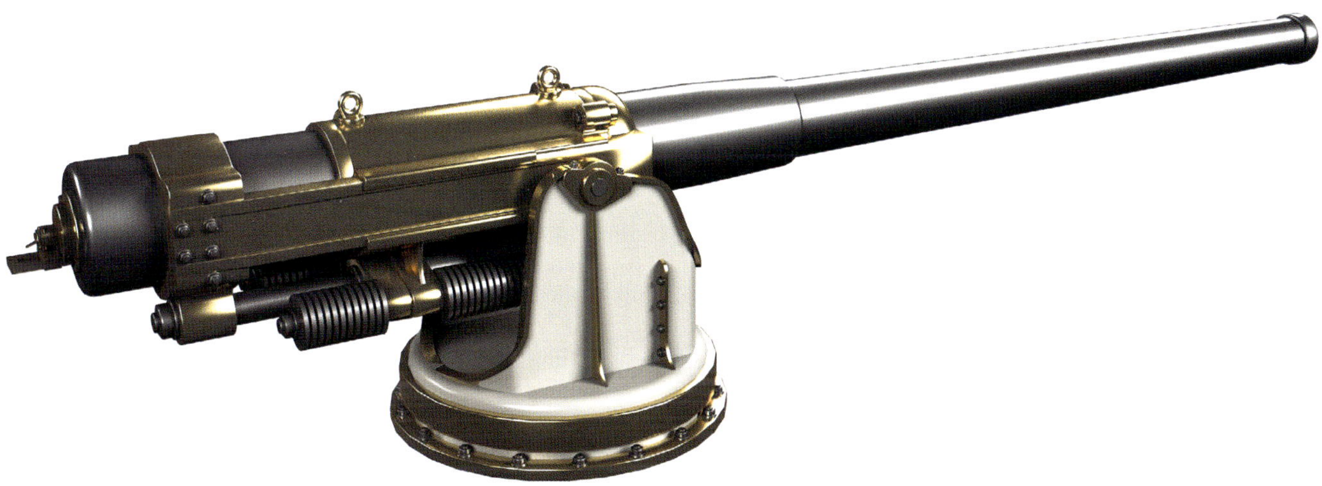

6 inch Canet gun.

3 inch Canet gun.

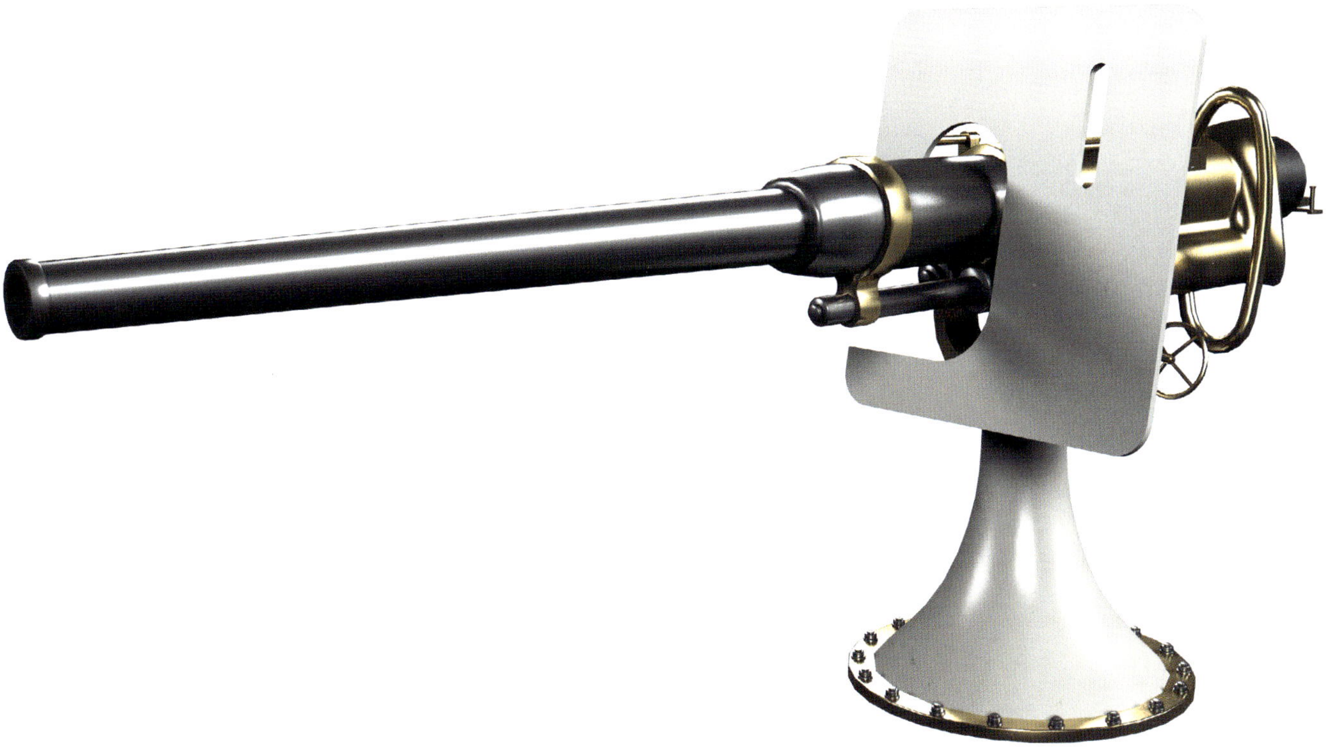

3 inch Canet gun.

Maxim 37mm automatic cannon (the initial design of the cruiser provided for the installation of two such guns).

Maxim 37mm automatic cannon (the initial design of the cruiser provided for the installation of two such guns).

47mm Hotchkiss cannon.

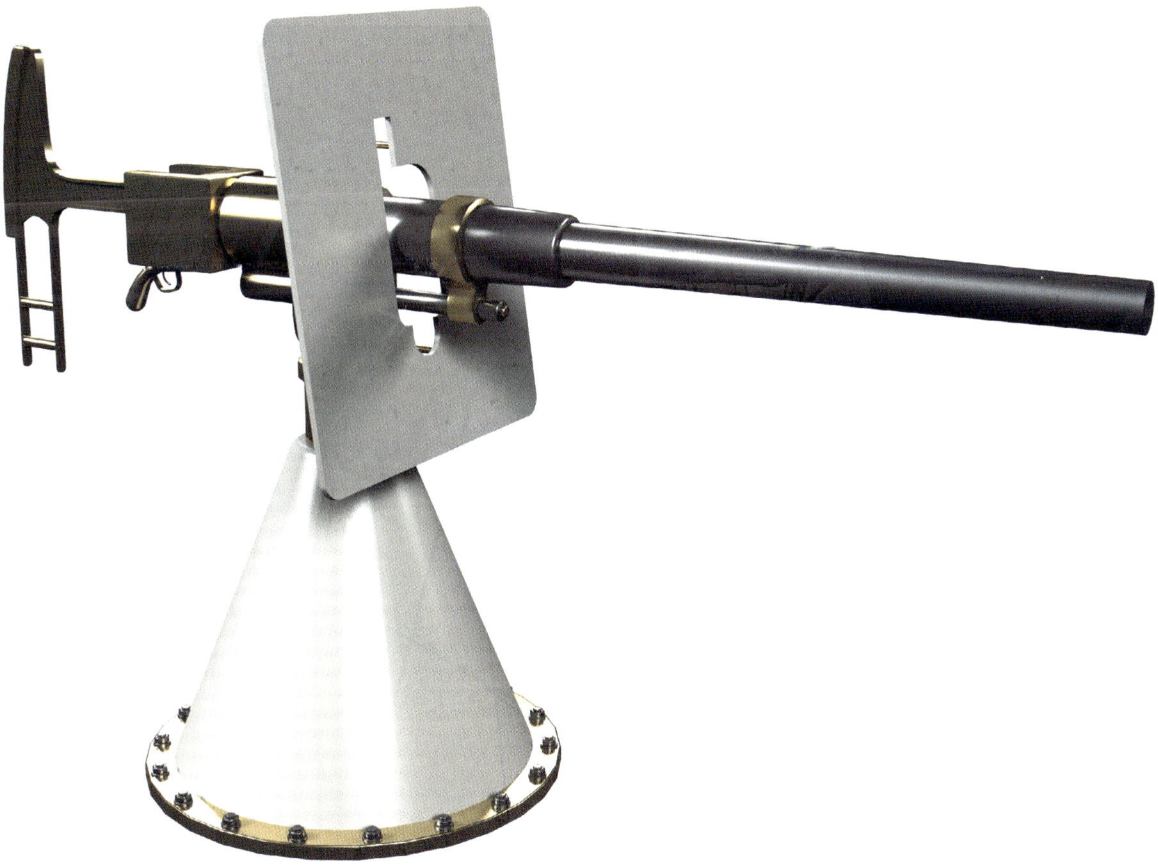

The Russian Cruiser Askold – Aliaksandr Sukhanevich

LUBLIN 2021 • ISBN 978-83-66673-76-2

3D illustrations and captions: **Aliaksandr Sukhanevich** • Text: **Jan Radziemski** • Text translation: **Piotr Kolasa** • Design: **KAGERO STUDIO** – Łukasz Maj

KAGERO Publishing • www.kagero.pl, e-mail: kagero@kagero.pl, marketing@kagero.pl, shop@kagero.pl

Editorial office, Marketing, Distribution: KAGERO Publishing, Akacjowa 100, os. Borek, Turka, 20-258 Lublin 62, Poland, phone/fax (+48) 81 501 21 05

w w w . k a g e r o . e u

3D visualisations are based on the available photographs, drawings and other archive data, and should be treated only as author's attempt to recreate the original look of the particular machine as faithfully as possible. If you are in possession of materials to which author did not reach, and you would like to help us to develop a better publication, please contact the Publisher on: redakcja@kagero.pl